King of Infinite Space

poems by

Anna Priddy

Finishing Line Press
Georgetown, Kentucky

King of Infinite Space

Copyright © 2023 by Anna Priddy
ISBN 979-8-88838-256-1 First Edition
All rights reserved under International and Pan-American Copyright Conventions. No part of this book may be reproduced in any manner whatsoever without written permission from the publisher, except in the case of brief quotations embodied in critical articles and reviews.

ACKNOWLEDGMENTS

Thank you to Jeffrey Levine and Kirsten Miles and all the good people at the Tupelo Press 30/30 Project and the friends who supported my efforts while I wrote these poems.

Publisher: Leah Huete de Maines
Editor: Christen Kincaid
Cover Art: Hadley Kronick
Author Photo: Amelia Blackmon
Cover Design: Elizabeth Maines McCleavy

Order online: www.finishinglinepress.com
also available on amazon.com

Author inquiries and mail orders:
Finishing Line Press
PO Box 1626
Georgetown, Kentucky 40324
USA

Table of Contents

Enter Ghost 1
Enter Ghost 2 2
Our State to be Disjoint or out of Frame 3
Get Thee to a Nunnery 4
Except my Life, Except my Life, Except my Life 5
Give Every Man Thy Ear, But Few Thy Voice 6
Words, Words, Words 7
The King of Infinite Space 8
The Play's the Thing 9
A Prince out of your Star 10
We Defy Augury 11
In My Youth I Suffered Much Extremity for Love 12
They Did Make Love to This Appointment 13
These are but Wild and Whirling Words 14
I am Too Much in the Sun 15
Your Noble Son is Mad 16
I Eat the Air 17
More than Kin and Less than Kind 18
A Mote it is to Trouble the Mind's Eye 19
A Mote it is to Trouble the Mind's Eye, II 20
The Undiscovered Country 21
These Blazes you Must Not Take for Fire 22
One May Smile, and Smile, and be a Villain 23
The World is a Prison 24
Now Could I Drink Hot Blood 25
I Must be Cruel Only to be Kind 26
The Interim's Mine 27
Exit Ghost 28

For Hadley and Alexander

Enter Ghost

The dead are always with us, just beyond
the outskirts of our minds, stalking
the parapet. Sometimes no more than
a scent, the smell of old wood, smoke, the cold,
a cigarette, and then, full blown, battle
ready, at the peak of all powers, there.
Stay, illusion. Did you usurp the night?
Did I climb to find you? Do you carry
portents or prophesies? I charge you speak.
You charge me speak. I've never known how.
A step toward; you recede. The cock crows.
I shall not look upon his like again.

Enter Ghost II

Remember me. Remember the garden
where secure, I slept. There slick poison
poured out into my ear, moving swiftly
into my throat. I was overtaken.
Remember me, lying on green velvet,
eyes closed, and he sat, perched near.
Rest, he said. I replied, *I wanted you
to like me.* And he, *Like you? I adore
you.* And it was the word *adore*, moving
into the ear that closed the eyes. How large,
a word to stop time, how monumental.
Long quiet and then a hand soft against
the face, brushing back the hair, so warm.
Two acts intwined, so that to close the eyes,
summons back the hand. There the soft touch,
there its heat. Remember me, said the ghost.
Three times he said it, and then, swear, swear, swear.

Our State to be Disjoint or out of Frame

Something is rotten here. Too much gone slack,
dissolution and isolation, back
in the before time when there were people,
when there was light and music and tables
to gather round and ankles and knees touched
beneath, elbows and hands above, gone now
are the times when we laughed, when a glance
could ignite an adventure. When the night
was full of promise and guitar players
played the blues, but offered joy in darkness.
Their fingers moved so quick to stir the blood.
The life and the sound and the fingering,
building and building, moving to something.
Now nothing stirs. On a chaise, in soft clothes,
The days go. Is it a judgement, a price
to be paid for the wastes of long ago?
Or the inevitable ugliness
of life slowing down, some rotting to come?

Get Thee to a Nunnery

Would you love me if you knew all of me?
That is, all about me, the lies I tell,
the ugly things I've done. In orisons
let all my sins be numbered. Who is that
who could know us full through and love us?
I have been a child and a girl, and where
is one who could have seen what I have seen,
or see what I see? I did love you
once. But also, he and he and he. Sin.
I say we shall have no more marriages.
Shall I lie in your lap? Lie to your face?
Shall I lie among the lilies along
the river's edge while the riven water
washes over me? Will you tell us what
the show meant? You are naught. I'll mark the play.

Except my Life, Except my Life, Except my Life

Nothing is important. If it is waste,
it has been, at times, completely my own,
and so mine to waste. And the great question
of being, answered only by the breath
keeping to its habit. How I love it.
When a child I was like a prisoner,
counting down the days, hoping to survive.
I wished and prayed, prayed and wished,
talking to fairies, then gods, to myself,
to whosoever might save me. None did.
I saved myself. Me, and time. Enemy
Time. Which is no respecter of persons.
And does cruel things to me. That currency
I can't get back, or hoard, nor hold on to.

Give Every Man Thy Ear, But Few Thy Voice

Every day I love it a bit more.
As for men, I have no interest there.
Dead men though, dead men I like, and the words
they left for me stir the blood and the mind,
as if increase of appetite had grown
by what it fed on. My ear, I will keep,
but my voice I give to everyone.

Words, Words, Words

To be or not to be comes down in part
to a question of words versus actions,
whether 'tis nobler to speak or not,
as when at birth that first intake of air
is followed by a scream. Does sound
equal life? The poet I loved more than life
used to say that one had to choose between
the life and the work. One lifetime is only
enough time to perfect one. He chose work.
Young, I thought, I can do both. And older,
I choose life. And older still, wondered why
he didn't say that both are impossible,
neither can be perfected; we're bumbling
through. But we believe words will outlast time.
When I read his poems I hear his voice.
Still here, though I would trade them for his life.
To all those endless freshman composition
students I say *essay* derives from French
essayer, which means to attempt or try.
Every essay should be an attempt
to say something. This is an attempt.

The King of Infinite Space

But that I have bad dreams. Why, just last night,
whole kingdoms slipped away while I lie trapped
in a fluorescent hospital room, drugged
and unable to move. The corridors were dark,
but noisy, with cart's wheels squeaking, machines
beeping, but no voices. My mind went down
the hall, all dark. I was the only one,
solitary patient in an empty
place. No one was coming to help me.
Without speech, unable to scream,
but screaming, screaming with no sound coming.
Only mind trapped in a nutshell body,
bounded by self with no help. Did nothing.
We know what we are, not what we may be.

The Play's the Thing

And here's this: how it perpetuates its
self, moving through all our selves. Once, a girl,
it comprised nearly all my life, just that
and the pain I could recount to no one.
Cried at the injustice, the boys shirtless
all summer, while I at age four was forced
to go about covered, uncomfortably
different. Complained until my mother
gave up; had maybe two months of bare
brown skin to match my bare feet, nothing but
pull-on polyester shorts, like a boy,
free to play. It's exhilarating,
that feeling, like one is moving toward
something raw and elemental, instinct,
maybe. It has to do with the body
and motion and the senses, a play
within a play. Grown, it comes rarely,
I sometimes seek it in the dark.

A Prince out of your Star

This is the very ecstasy of love,
that shutters the eyes to better breathe you
in and exalts at the scent and the sound,
breath comingling. Your air should be my air.
Out of orbit and out of reach, above
and not below me. I cannot see you,
but I saw you once, and that was enough.

We Defy Augury

Today is all coated in ice, slickly
dangerous and dripping. Would that each drop
foretold an ending. Or a beginning.
But that downward motion tends to the ground,
where all things end. I count myself among
the lucky ones. Nothing can touch me here.
I am the fattened calf, the golden child,
forever beautiful, the thing itself.
That's one version. You can find another
by asking someone else. Repeatedly,
as a child, I was warned about getting
above my raising. And then once told cream
cannot help but rise to the very top.
There may be another version written
in the stars, or in the Master's great book,
the one that subtracts out agency.
A forgone conclusion. I cannot say.

In My Youth I Suffered Much Extremity for Love

Will you walk in the air? I could tell you
something. My cheeks grow hot, just as they did
when I was twenty. Touch the memory.
I knew him well. Twenty-four hours I drove
without rest just to reach the place his scent
would be. Wrapped in his sheets,
in a wooden bed, atop a wooden
stair, in a wooden house, in New England
woods. Though this be madness without method,
here are some things I did: I started when
he said my name; I noted the passing
of his car; I caught his eyes with mine,
held his stare. I read the books he assigned;
I fell to my knees in tears. I yielded.
There is nothing like love for a man,
especially when he is dead. I call
a number that means nothing to no one.
In my desk I keep the key to his door.
He doesn't live at that place anymore.

They Did Make Love to This Appointment

Off they go. Summers in Massachusetts
are rare. There is a certain slant of light
and a heat just right, it's as if a life
could be lived in open air. I was young.
There were fireworks in July, and an arm
around me, and oh, I was proud to be
held by a man. There was a beautiful
red-haired girl, older, who took me around,
treated me like I was grown. Christopher,
who clambered up to the open window
of my rented room when I was too drunk
to find my keys. All was open windows
and nights full of promise to walk through.

These are but Wild and Whirling Words

I am just doing the best that I can
with what I have. Blue and pink cloud feathers
lay strewn across the sky this morning, while
the moon unperceptively took her leave,
going in the dark. It's bracing cold, early,
but there are appointments to keep, moving
along familiar roads. From my mind
I'll wipe away all other memory.
Sometimes there is such joy. And then those gone
before us like the sun. Thou needs no ghost,
my lord, come from the grave to tell us this.
We walk first in sun and then in sorrow.
Words are not the currency of the dead;
the words whirl in the minds of the living,
phrases that once held meaning, divorced
from shared experience, *I'll be along,*
but how will I find you when I get there?

I am Too Much in the Sun

Whole summers I gave over to just this:
A towel spread on concrete next to chain-link
fencing at my head and a public pool
at my feet, and novels, so many books.
At least one year my mind was in Russia
while my body remained in Kentucky.
I willed my life away. Heat on my skin
and refusal of food made me feel like
a saint, some grand ascetic. If I think back,
I'm still conflicted. Then I wavered, thought
both that I was horrid, with a story
to ugly to tell or carry—and then
that I was magic, slim and brown and fine.
And here's the problem, when you're in the sun
too long and you stand, turn, or move,
nothing looks right. If I look at her now,
I still can't make up my mind what is true:
am I exactly that same girl, or if
she's someone I no longer recognize.

Your Noble Son Is Mad

When day is day, night-night, and time is time,
then all will be right, but who is to say,
what is time, or day, or night? Golden boys,
who start out with such beauty and promise,
and then, the slip of a record's needle,
a fever dream, the wrong drug, a ghost's walk,
and all is lost. I was full of envy,
thought my brother, my sister better loved,
thought every other child better placed,
thought every person superior, thought
every boy too good for me. Especially
him, all music and antic disposition,
who did not believe in madness, only
poetry. But I thought something was wrong
with me. He pushed me beyond all borders;
though I was scared, I learned, I am but mad
north-northwest, when the wind is southerly,
I know a hawk from a handsaw. I know
the day and the night and the time, how much
life was lost with your son. Alone here it's
all southerly wind, hawkish sanity.

I Eat the Air

Promise crammed, like the echo of a line
from Plath. I can exist on anything.
What is to come, what has been, even crumbs.
Wormwood. Only after it was brought home,
finding resin-like drippings on the floor,
learned that meant it was no good, that worms bore
through, eating the wood from the inside out.
I could interpret between you, your love
if I could see the puppets dallying.
You could show me. Turn yourself inside out.

More than Kin and Less than Kind

It's said there is nothing good or bad but
thinking makes it so. Yet, there are bad things,
aren't there? Don't let me come too close to it—
Family is a nightmare to escape,
if escape were possible. In one way
the mind can arrange it, and distance, death,
but not really. It's a double-helix
rune, a Larkinian shelf, a cage
of blood and bone, a story written down.
It is, mostly, a trap. A conclusion.
Think your way out of it. Move far away.
Die, if you will, but it is still all yours,
as sure as a sword striking its appointed
mark, stage directions playing themselves out.

A Mote it is to Trouble the Mind's Eye

Surrounding all sides of the world's prison,
dropping over us like freezing rainfall,
insinuating itself between sheets,
worming its way into bodies wishing
for dreamless sleep, the ghost of our father
spreads its arms. What to make of the vision?
A harbinger it must be, but of what?
The unthinkable that seeks out us all,
here in full battle dress, its full powers.
Closing the eyes does not will it away.
Does it mean the entire kingdom will fall?
As far as ourselves are concerned, it does.

A Mote it Is to Trouble the Mind's Eye, II

But to see him here as he was in life
is a remarkable thing all the same.
A dream itself is but a shadow, no
substance to be found. Reaching out you find
your hand passes through. And we do not know
what dreams may come, nor can we bid this one
stay, or seek the place where it may be found.
Whether under the cold, unyielding ground,
in the firmament, a dimension slipped
just beyond this one, matters not to me.
What matters is I cannot touch him.

The Undiscovered Country

Should also be a part of infinite space,
but that is the territory from which
no traveler returns, excepting those
two poets. I would go there for you, love.
Until China and Africa meet, 'til
the seven stars go squawking, I go there
in my mind and seek you out. I cannot
find you. God knows, I cannot bring you back.
Those two, their beloveds, their art, even
so, could traverse and map the place, but failed
to bring anyone back. Could not overcome.
There is no looking back, but there's the map,
the map cast into the past.
There is special providence in the fall
of a sparrow, like the fall of a tear.

These Blazes you Must Not Take for Fire

In the midst of flames, may you find yourself
burning, burning, with the heat sinking in
even unto your bones. May you find your
body, turning, to take in the color
that changes and moves and will not stay still,
taking in, in the flames, with all senses,
color, heat, sound, the sweet smell of woodsmoke
that is in your eyes, mouth, and on your tongue,
in your hair and your skin, enveloping,
encompassing, closing in, in the midst
of flames, may you find yourself, saying, I
am native here and to the manner born.

One May Smile, and Smile, and be a Villain

One may be the villain and still not know.
Don't we all feel we've done the best we could?
In that is forgiveness, because we must
believe that all people are, all the time,
doing the best they can with what they have
and know at the time. Near to my conscience
are the things I do not know, nearer still
the memory of the things I have done.
We sugar over the devil himself.

The World Is a Prison

And I do not mind; it's all I know.
There are more things in heaven and earth
than are dreamt of in your philosophy.
I would have liked to experience more.
There are places, I do not know their names,
I would have liked to travel. Here are walls
that enclose, and just outside the window
a little boy I made myself bounces
on his trampoline, in circles, netting
keeping him safe. He used to live in me.
Within and without, around, up and down,
and the springs' cry repeats, saying, here, here,
we are here, and we are glad to be here.

Now Could I Drink Hot Blood

Now it is winter, a full year fallow
gone by like so much waste. Everywhere death
slinks about, coming close enough to scare.
We are at a party, I sometimes say.
We arrive at birth, the party full swing.
It's so crowded, at first you learn only
the circle you can see. You move about.
Circle, settle, find your people, your loves.
Every minute people are leaving.
In truth even faster. You cannot know
the hour nor the day, and it is not fair.
And there are those who leave and take it all
with them, and there seems nothing left for you.
The party continues, though you are less
desirable a guest, like someone who
fed upon another, deprived of food.

I Must be Cruel Only to be Kind

Sharper than a serpent's tooth is the sting
of an ungrateful child, and they are all
ungrateful. And so it hurts—we each hurt.
Somewhere he keeps a catalog of wrongs
I have committed, all good goes begging.
Whatever I am to others, this crown,
is nothing to him, seeing only flaws.
They are many. I see them reflected
back to me in his visage, and like some
latter day Cleopatra, I hold him
close to my breast, love suffused with pain.

The Interim's Mine

The space between thought and word, a look
and the act, the blade and the flesh, the dash
between the beginning date and the end,
that belongs to me. Although a man's life be
no more than to say the word one, the pause
is pregnant with meaning. It can be found
in the after, the achieved conclusion.

Exit Ghost

The last words are Herbert's, from a gothic
classroom, tree covered, and these words, these
words, what can they do, what can they do, Prince.
That last hanging there in the air, almost
solid and so ponderous, calling him,
calling the boy back into being, boy,
my edition puts him at thirty, but
he remains a boy to me, innocence
lost. What more innocent than a classroom
and open, silent faces, listening,
hearing words that will walk with them all through
their lives. And so he was for a moment
like us, that prince, and his death was felt
and terrible. Some of us are dead now.
So is the one who told us the poem.
But the poem is still here, that shamed us
into silence as if we ourselves
were responsible for that misguided
end, all of us praying to be Hamlet,
not the one left to hurl a final word,
whatever its power, its importance.

Anna Priddy was born in Louisville, Kentucky, from whence she left immediately after high school for Mount Holyoke College. At Mount Holyoke, after some time writing fiction, she took a class on Lyric Poetry with Joseph Brodsky, and fell forever in love with poetry. She earned an MFA in Poetry Writing at Louisiana State University, as well as an MA and PhD in English. She is the author of two reference books: *How to Write about Emily Dickinson* and *How to Write about William Faulkner*. She has published scholarship on James Tate, Gjertrud Schnakenberg, Louise Gluck, Robert Penn Warren, Robert Lowell, and other writers. *King of Infinite Space* is her first chapbook.

www.ingramcontent.com/pod-product-compliance
Lightning Source LLC
Chambersburg PA
CBHW022126090426
42743CB00008B/1027